EMERALD GUIDES

MANAGING PERSONAL BANKRUPTCY

MANAGING THE PROCESS AND SURVIVING PERSONAL BANKRUPTCY IN ENGLAND AND WALES

DAVID MARSH

www.emeraldpublishing.co.uk

Emerald Guides
Brighton BN2 4EG

© Straightforward Publishing 2010

ISBN 9781847161581

Printed by GN Digital Printing Essex

Cover design by Straightforward Graphics

Contents

Alternatives to Bankruptcy

The Process of Bankruptcy

Introduction

This is a book that deals exclusively with personal bankruptcies and does not deal with company insolvencies. It also deals with alternatives to bankruptcy, such as Debt relief Orders and Individual Voluntary Arrangements-recognising that bankruptcy is the last and final option.

Over the last two years, personal bankruptcies have risen to record levels, in large part to do with the economic climate, i.e. recession and also the steady rise in personal debt over the last ten years or so, fuelled by an economic boom that has ended, as they all do, in tears. This time the end has resulted in the worst recession since the great depression of 1929.

It is predicted that in 2010 around 150,000 individuals will go bankrupt, up 12% on 2009. Relatively new to the ranks are a lot of professionals, such as lawyers and judges. More people are going for IVA's (Individual Voluntary Arrangements, see Chapter 3,). Many people are opting for the recently introduced Debt Relief Orders, which are cheap to enter into (£90 as opposed to £510 for personal bankruptcy) but applying only to those with less than £15,000 in debts and under £300 in assets (See Chapter 2). In addition, pensioners, once a negligible part of the whole picture, are increasingly having to seek relief from debt.

This very practical book offers a step-by-step guide to personal bankruptcy and also to alternatives to bankruptcy such as Debt Relief Orders, Individual Voluntary Arrangements, Administration Orders, and the more informal Debt Management Plans. The book starts by looking at the insolvency service and who's who in the world of bankruptcy, including the role of the official receiver.

The nature and type of advice available to people who are considering bankruptcy is covered. How to deal with creditors and also institutions such as banks is also covered along with the process of bankruptcy, costs, the hearing and the bankruptcy petition plus the interview with the Official receiver.

Following the process of bankruptcy, the duties and restrictions imposed upon an individual are covered along with the eventual discharge from bankruptcy. The nature of debts included in the bankruptcy process are covered along with the treatment of assets.

Overall, this is a very practical book, complete with key forms used in the bankruptcy process. Any individual who is contemplating bankruptcy will benefit directly from the practical advice contained within.

Chapter One

The Personnel Involved in Bankruptcy

The Insolvency Service

The Insolvency Service operates under a statutory framework-mainly the Insolvency Acts 1986 and 2000, the Company Directors Disqualifications Act 1986 and the Employment Rights Act 1996. There are a network of 38 Official Receiver offices throughout England and Wales. The Enforcement Directorate and headquarters are in London, Birmingham, Manchester and Edinburgh.

What the Insolvency Service does

The Insolvency Service:

- administers and investigates the affairs of bankrupts, of companies and partnerships wound up by the court, and establishes why they became solvent;
- acts as trustee/liquidator where no private sector insolvency practitioner is appointed;
- acts as nominee and supervisor in fast-track individual voluntary arrangements;
- takes forward reports of bankrupts' and directors misconduct;
- deals with the disqualification of unfit directors in all corporate failures;

- deals with bankruptcy restriction orders and undertakings;
- authorises and regulates the insolvency profession;
- assesses and pays statutory entitlement to redundancy payments when an employer cannot or will not pay its employees;
- provides banking and investment services for bankruptcy and liquidation estate funds;
- advises BIS ministers and other government departments and agencies on insolvency, redundancy and related issues;
- provides information to the public on insolvency and redundancy matters via its helpline 0845 602 9848, website, www.insolvency.gov.uk, Leaflets and Redundancy Payments Helpline.

The Insolvency Service also carries out investigations into companies.

If you are thinking about going bankrupt you should contact the Insolvency Service on their helpline-addresses also contained in the back of this book.

The Official Receiver

The Official Receiver is a civil servant in the Insolvency Service and an Officer of the Court. He or she will be notified by the court of the bankruptcy or winding up order. He will then be responsible through his staff for administering the initial stage, at least, of the insolvency case. This stage includes collecting and protecting any assets and investigating the causes of the bankruptcy or winding up.

The Official Receiver's staff will contact you, either immediately if action is urgently needed or within 2 days of receiving an insolvency order or bankruptcy order. Usually they will arrange an appointment for you to attend the Official Receiver's office for an interview, normally within ten working days of receiving the order from the court. He or she will then act as your trustee in bankruptcy unless the court appoints an insolvency practitioner to take this role. Assuming that it is the Official Receiver who will be acting as your trustee, he or she will be responsible for looking after your financial affairs during your bankruptcy and also your financial affairs prior to you being made bankrupt.

If the Official receiver does not require you to attend an interview you will be sent a questionnaire to fill in and return. See chapter three for the detailed process of bankruptcy and the steps involved.

ALTERNATIVES TO BANKRUPTCY

Chapter 2

Debt Relief Orders

Before considering going down the road of bankruptcy, there are a number of viable alternatives, one of which may suit you. These alternatives are based on a person being solvent and having enough surplus income to pay off debts, or a proportion of debts, over a specified period. In most cases, with the exceptions of Debt Management Plans, the alternatives are ratified by the courts, administered by third parties and provide relief from creditors. In addition, any surplus debts after the expiry of the order are then written off.

Debt Management Plans are somewhat different and more personal, are not legal although can be administered by a third party. We will be discussing these at the end of this chapter.

Debt Relief Orders

What is a debt Relief Order?

A debt relief order, which came into force in April 2009, is an order you can apply for if you can't afford to pay off your debts. It is granted by the Insolvency Service and is a cheaper option than going bankrupt.

You must have debts of less than £15,000 and a low income to apply for a debt relief order. It usually lasts for one year and, during that time, none of the people that you owe money to (creditors) will be able to take action against you to get their money back. At the end of the year you will be free of all the debts listed in the order. You can't apply for a debt relief order if you:

- own things of value or have savings of over £300

- Own a vehicle worth more than £1,000

- Have a private pension fund worth over £300

To apply for a debt relief order, you will need to contact an authorised advisor who will check whether or not you meet the specific conditions and then applies for the order on your behalf. Details of authorised advisors can be obtained from the Insolvency Service, the Law Society or from a Citizens Advice Bureau. The order will cost you £90 but you can pay this in instalments over six-months.

Who can apply for a debt relief order?

You can only apply for a debt relief order if you meet certain conditions. These are when:

- You have qualifying debts of £15,000 or over. These debts must be of a certain type

- You have disposable income of less than £150 per month after expenses (normal expenses). When you work out this figure you must take into account all of the money that you have coming into your household. This includes salary and wages, any benefits, pension, contributions from other household members and any rental income.

- The assets that you own and any savings are worth less than £300. Your motor vehicle must be worth less than £1,000 unless it has been specially adapted because you have a physical disability.

- In the last three years you must have lived, had a property or carried on a business in England or Wales.

Type of debts included in a debt relief order

As explained, only certain types of debts can be included in a debt relief order. These are termed qualifying debts and include:

- Credit cards
- Overdrafts
- Loans
- Rent
- Utilities
- Telephone
- Council tax
- Benefit overpayments
- Social fund loans
- Hire purchase or conditional sale agreements
- Buy now-pay later agreements

Certain types of loans cannot be included such as:
- Court fines and confiscation orders-basically fines relating to criminal activity

- Child support and maintenance
- Student loans

Your assets

Assets are the things of value that you own. As explained above, if you own assets worth more than £300, or if you have a motor vehicle worth more than £1,000 you won't be able to apply for a debt relief order. Examples of assets that you may own include savings, vehicles, shares, antiques, and property. This is not an exhaustive list. Essentially, anything with a value can be counted as an asset.

In relation to property, if you own a property it is very unlikely that you can apply for a Debt Relief Order. The fact that you may have a mortgage on it will not matter.

If you have not reached retirement age, but have a private or occupational pension fund, then the value of the fund counts towards the £300 limit. If you have retired and are receiving payments from a pension, then this will be regarded as income rather than an asset.

When working out what is an asset, and the value of an asset, there are some items that you don't have to take into account. These include:

- Household equipment such as bedding clothing and furniture, i.e. essential items.

- Tools, books and any other item of equipment that you may use in your business

- A car which has been specially adapted because you have a physical disability and which you need to carry out your everyday activities.

- A motor vehicle worth less than £1,000.

Those ineligible for a debt relief order

A person cannot get a debt relief order if the following applies:

- Person currently bankrupt

- You have an IVA (Individual Voluntary Arrangement) or are applying for an IVA.

- Creditors have applied to make you bankrupt but the hearing hasn't yet taken place. You might still be able to apply for a debt relief order if your creditors agree.

- You have been given a bankruptcy restrictions order or undertaking.

- You have petitioned for bankruptcy but your petition has not yet been dealt with.

- You have had a Debt Relief Order in the last six years.

- You have been given a debt relief restriction order or undertaking.

Applying for a Debt Relief Order

Debt relief orders are administered by the Official Receiver through the Insolvency Service. However, you can only apply for a debt relief order through a third party or intermediary and not through the Insolvency Service Direct. An intermediary is usually a skilled debt advisor who has been permission to proceed with the advice and paperwork. Intermediaries can be found by going to the Citizens Advice Service website www. Citizensadvice.org.uk. You can also find intermediaries through contacting the Insolvency Service www.insolvency.gov.uk

As mentioned above the cost of applying for a debt relief order is £90, which must be paid in cash at a payzone outlet. A list of these outlets can be found at www.payzone.co.uk. The £90 can be paid in six-monthly instalments. However, the Official receiver won't consider an application until the fee has been paid in full. The fee is non-refundable. It is an offence to give false or misleading statements in your application. Once the debt relief order has been approved then you shouldn't pay any of the creditors listed in the order. Your creditors will be informed about the order and they will be prevented from taking any action.

The debt relief order will be published on the Individual Insolvency Register at www.insolvency.gov.uk. The register is available to the public. Your name and address will remain on the register for 15 months.

Things not to do before applying for a DRO or during the order

There are certain things that you cannot do either before you apply for a DRO or during the life of the DRO. Mainly:

- You cannot hide, destroy or falsify any books or documents up to one year before you apply for an order and during the order period
- You must tell the Official Receiver of any changes in your circumstances that would affect the application between making the application and the order being granted
- You cannot give away or sell things for less than they are worth to help you get a debt relief order.

If you are found guilty of doing any of the above you will be committing an offence which could prevent you obtaining an order or fined or imprisoned. If you have already been granted a debt relief order then the Official receiver can apply for a Debt Relief Restriction Order or the debt relief order might be taken away.

During the Debt Relief Order period

During the period of a Debt Relief Order you won't have to pay towards the debts listed in the order. The creditors of these debts cannot take any action against you. A Debt Relief Order normally lasts 12 months.

However, as listed above there are certain debts that can't be included in a DRO. These include normal household expenses including rent, utilities and council tax. You will also have to pay off any debts that are not included in the order. New debts cannot be added once an order is made. You have to tell the Official Receiver about any new debts incurred or if you have forgotten to include any new debts in the order.

Your debt relief order will appear on your credit file and remain on there for six years. This may affect your credit in the future and you might find it difficult to open a bank account.

With a Debt Relief Order in place, there are certain things that you cannot do. These are called 'restrictions' and include the following:

- Getting credit over £500 without telling the lender you have a DRO

- Carrying on a business in a different name from the one under which you were given a DRO

- Being involved with promoting, managing or setting up a limited company, without permission from court.

If the Official receiver believes that you have provided wrong information or have been dishonest they can apply for a Debt Relief Restriction Order. If you are given a Debt Relief Restriction Order, this means that the restrictions on the things that you can do can last from 2-15 years. However, the DRO will still end 12 months after being granted and you won't have to pay off any debts listed in the order. If you don't follow the restrictions you will be committing an offence.

Changes in circumstances

You have the responsibility to inform the Official Receiver of any changes in your circumstances during the period of the DRO. This includes any assets of real value that you acquire during the DRO, e.g. money that has been left you. Failure to inform the Official Receiver might mean the cancelling of your DRO and you will then be responsible for all debts listed in the DRO.

Chapter 3

Individual Voluntary Arrangements

An Individual Voluntary Arrangement (IVA) is a formal agreement between you and your creditors where you will come to an arrangement with people you owe money to, to make reduced payments towards the total amount of your debt in order to pay off a percentage of what you owe then generally after 5 years your debt is classed as settled.

Due to its formal nature, an IVA has to be set up by a licensed professional. You should first go to the official insolvency website www.insolvencyhelpline.co.uk or phone the UK Insolvency Helpline for more information (0845 602 9848) to source a licensed Insolvency Practitioner. Many firms have jumped on the insolvency bandwagon in the last few years. However, unlike these firms, the Licensed Insolvency Practitioners on the panel do not charge any fees up front for putting together a client's proposals for an Individual Voluntary Arrangement.

How IVA's work

Once a Licensed Insolvency Practitioner has made a decision that an IVA is the correct instrument for you to solve your debt problems, you will then be asked questions regarding your current financial situation. This is an in-depth interview, and, based on the information that you give, a debt repayment plan will be drawn up.

To qualify for an IVA one or more of the following criteria must apply to your situation:

- You must have mounting debts of several thousand pounds or more

- The bulk of your debts must be unsecured

- You must have a regular income

- You are presently employed

- You can supply verification of income

Based on this information, with an assessment of income and outgoings a plan can be drawn up for you. You must scrutinise this plan and then sign it if you agree, or discuss it if you don't.

An application may then be made to court for an interim order. Once this order is in place, no creditors will be able to take legal action against you. Following the grant of this order the Nominee (Licensed Insolvency Practitioner) will circulate to the creditors the following information:

- The Nominee's comments on the debtor's proposals

- The proposals

- Notice of the date and location of the meeting of creditors to vote on the proposals

- A statement of affairs-this effectively being a list of the assets and the liabilities of the debtor

- A schedule advising creditors of the requisite majority required to approve the IVA

- A complete list of creditors

- A guide to the fees charged by the supervisor following the approval of the IVA

- A form of proxy for voting purposes

A creditor meeting will then take place at which you should attend.

For an IVA to be approved, creditors will be called on to vote either for or against the arrangement. If only one creditor votes "for" the IVA, the IVA will be approved. However, if only one creditor votes against the IVA, and they represent less than 25% of your total debt, the meeting will be suspended until a later date, and other creditors who did not vote will be called on to vote.

If the creditor who voted against the IVA represents more than 25% of the total debt you owe then the IVA will fail. This is because an IVA will only ever be approved if 75% in monetary value is voted for. If any of the creditor's don't vote it is assumed that they will vote for the IVA.

The IVA will be legally binding. As long as you keep up the repayments, when the term of your agreement is finished, you will be free from these debts regardless of how much has been paid off. During the period of the arrangement your financial situation will be reviewed regularly to see if there are any changes in your circumstances.

It is worth noting that if you do enter into an IVA with your creditors and have an endowment policy linked to your mortgage, or equity in your property or a pension fund then these will be taken into account when working out income/assets/outgoings.

Key components for a successful IVA

- The IVA must offer a higher return to creditors than could otherwise be expected were the debtor to be made bankrupt.

- An honest declaration of your assets and/or anticipated future earnings should be made. Material or false declarations are very likely to result in an unsuccessful IVA.

Advantages of an IVA

Individual, partner or sole trader

- Enables a sole trader or partner to continue to trade and generate income towards repayment to creditors.

- No restrictions in regards to personal credit although in practice can be hard to obtain.

- The proposals are drawn up by the debtor and are entirely flexible to accommodate personal circumstances.

- The debtor does not suffer the restrictions imposed by bankruptcy, such as not being able to operate as a director of a limited company etc.

- The costs of administering an IVA are considerably lower than in bankruptcy, enabling a higher return to creditors.

- IVA's operate as an insolvency procedure and creditors can as a consequence of this, still reclaim tax and VAT relief as a bad debt.

Disadvantages of an IVA

- Where contributions from income are being made, IVA's are generally expected to be for a period longer than bankruptcy, i.e. 5 years as opposed to 1 year.

- If the debtor fails to comply with the terms of the arrangement his home and assets can still be at risk if they have not been specifically excluded from the proposals.

- If the IVA fails as a consequence of the debtor not meeting obligations, it is likely that the debtor will be made bankrupt at this time.

- There will be no opportunity for a trustee in bankruptcy to investigate the actions of the debtor or possibility of hidden assets.

Chapter 4

Administration Orders

An Administration Order is a single county court order that covers all eligible debts and rolls them up together. A single payment is made every month into the court. The court staff then divides the payment up amongst creditors on a pro-rata basis. Like other court orders, an Administration Order stops creditors from taking further or separate action against you.

Rolling up your eligible debts into an administration order can save you a lot of time and also stress as the court will deal with your debts on your behalf. Any interest and other charges that were being added onto your debts are automatically stopped on the granting of an Administration Order.

There is no initial up-front fee for an Administration Order. The court takes a fee of 10 pence out of every pound owed, which means that the handling fee is 10% of your overall debts. The fee is deducted from payments into court. If you apply for a composition order at the same time that you apply for the Administration Order then the amount of time that you make payments for is limited, usually to three years. This is because, if you are paying only a very small amount to your creditors then the order could go on for years. A Composition Order is a way of making sure that this does not happen. If the judge does decide to make a Composition Order then this is usually limited to three years, meaning that you will have to pay off part of your debts only.

If you do not have a Composition Order in place, you can apply for one separately even after your Administration Order is in effect. This can be applied for using form N244.

Who is eligible to apply for an Administration Order?

You can get an Administration order if:

- You have at least two debts.

- Have at least one county court or High Court Judgement against you.

- The total of your debts is less than £5,000.

If you are seeking an Administration Order you can apply on form N92, obtainable online or from your local county court. The form has notes to help you in the completion. The first page of the form will ask you to list all of your debts. It is important that this is completed thoroughly, together with any arrears on priority debts. You should not sign the form at this stage. You need to take it to the county court and sign the declaration in front of a court officer. Always keep a copy of the form.

Once the court has accepted your application, your creditors will be automatically informed that you have applied for an Administration Order. Your creditors then have 16 days in which to lodge any objections that they may have, for example, they may consider that the payments offered are too low. Your creditors can also ask the court to not include them in the Order. Certain creditors, priority creditors, will almost certainly object, such as mortgage, utilities (gas and electricity), as they will want to reach their own arrangements with you.

If no objections are received within 16 days, and the courts are happy with what you have offered, then the Administration Order will be made. The creditors can take no further action provided that you pay what you have offered on time. If there is a problem, then the order should not be refused without a court hearing. A hearing should be arranged at court for you and you should always attend, or write to the court if your reason for non-attendance is valid. Once the order is in place you make your payment to the court and not the creditors.

The Administration Order will last until the debts are paid in full, unless a Composition Order is made. Either the creditors can ask for a review of the order at any time or you can apply to amend it in the light of changing circumstances. Details of the Administration Order are recorded on credit reference files for a period of six years from the date of the order.

Debts

Most courts will expect all of your debts to be listed on the forms, including priority debts such as mortgage. You will need to state whether the debts are in joint names and list them. Joint debts can cause problems as, because there is joint and several liability the creditors can still go after them. If the other person also has a court order against them and debts of less than £5,000 they can still apply for a separate Administration Order.

One important point to note is that your application may be refused if the information given reveals that you haven't got enough money to pay what you have offered.

Other factors involved in applying for an Administration Order

Certain debts are treated differently to the most common debts. Council tax arrears for previous years can be included in the Administration Order but not the current years bill, unless the council has told you that you have lost the right to pay in instalments and must pay the balance in one lump sum.

Magistrate's court fines can be included in the application but the judge may leave them out. Any social fund loans and benefit overpayments are left out, as they are not ordinary debts.

No longer able to afford payments?

If you find yourself in a position where you can no longer keep up with the terms of the order then you can apply to change the amount that you pay each month. You can use a N244 form and there shouldn't be a fee. You should state that you are applying for a variation of payments you are making under your Administration Order and say why you are applying. You should attach a copy of a personal budget sheet to indicate how you have arrived at the revised figures. The meeting to discuss amendments will be with a District Judge who can make any changes needed. If you don't keep up with the payments in the order then the court can cancel or revoke the Administration Order. If this happens your creditors can then pursue you for the debts.

Administration Order paid off?

When you have paid the Order off in full you can get a Certificate of Satisfaction from the county court. There is a fee for this, currently £15. Details of your Administration Order are kept by the Registry of County Court Judgements and by credit reference agencies. These agencies will mark your file to indicate that the debt has been paid off.

If you have a Composition Order on your Administration Order then you can still get a Certificate of Satisfaction to show that the Administration Order has been paid but individual debts will not be marked as satisfied as they have not been paid in full. However, none of the creditors on the Administration Order can take action against you either because it has been paid in full or paid the amount owed under the Composition order.

****

Chapter 5

Debt Management Plans

A Debt Management Plan is a way of planning your debt payments over a number of years. It has similarities to an Individual Voluntary Arrangement in that it is a way of organising and paying off debt and keeping creditors at bay.

There are two types of Debt Management Plan:

1. The type where you are provided with standard letters and you are in charge of making payments. With this method you are in charge of dealing with your creditors.

2. The type where a third party contacts all your creditors. Using this method, your financial situation is illustrated by a set of papers called a common financial statement. You will be represented by a third party and given 24hr support.

Whichever way you go, the end result is to control your debts.

The debt management plans have no legal standing and are not ratified by a court, as is an Administration Order for example.

A debt management plan can provide solutions for the following:

- Those with unsecured debts that they cannot afford to pay

- Those with equity in their properties but who would rather not re-mortgage or take out a loan
- Those who do not qualify for an IVA, i.e. those with debts under £12,000

- For people who want a short term solution to debts i.e. those who are about to sell a home

- People who don't want to deal with their debts but would rather a third party take this on.

Essentially, a Debt Management Plan places your debt with a third party who deals with your debts on your behalf. Debt Management Plans are far more effective than taking out unregulated loans with very high rates of interest. It is very important to remember that debts with underlying security in them cannot be put into a plan.

Examples of unsecured borrowing

- Personal loans
- Overdrafts
- Credit cards
- Student loans
- Store cards

Secured borrowing is where the lender has a legal charge over some property of yours, so that if you default on payments, they can possess that property and sell it to get their money back.

Generally...

The length of time that the debt management plan runs will depend on the way it is structured. A simple approach is to divide your debts into what your monthly payments are and that is the number of months that the plan will run.

When organising the Plan you should concentrate on the priority of your debts. A priority debt is one which can have serious results if not paid, such as mortgage, utilities etc. Some loans may be secured against your home so these would be treated as priority. You will need to look carefully at your spending and cut down unnecessary expenditure. All of us have to do this, particularly in recession. Look to get cheaper deals on gas and electricity.

Beware that debt management companies, of which there are many, will charge a fee to carry out the planning and negotiating for you. The recession has provided the perfect opportunity for unscrupulous operators to target vulnerable people. When considering going down the road of a debt management plan you should contact a reputable operator, such as the Insolvency Helpline www.insolvency helpline.co.uk

Structuring a Debt Management Plan

Before you approach a debt management company you will need to collect together information about your financial affairs and follow some simple steps:

- Make a complete list of all your debts-divide them into separate headings such as priority and non-priority debts.

You will need to make offers to pay off your priority debts before tackling non-priority debts.

- The next step is to work out your income and expenditure. Be honest and make sure the amounts are realistic. What you are trying to do here is to gain a clear picture of your situation-which can be very beneficial.

- Contact your creditors and inform them that you are putting together a debt management plan.

- Do not borrow extra money to pay off your debts. Think about ways in which you can maximise your income-for example are you claiming all the benefits that you are entitled to.

It is very important, as stated above, that you inform your creditors that you are structuring your debt. They should then be on your side. However, as debt management plans have no legal standing, creditors do not have to accept them although, if it comes to court action against you then the fact that you have a plan will stand in your favour. Creditors are not allowed to harass you and if you are being harassed then you should contact an advice an agency, such as the Citizens Advice Bureau. It is important, once you have structured your plan, that you let your creditors have a copy so they can see what you are doing and, hopefully, agree to it.

Making payments

Most people will pay their debt management plans by standing order through their bank account. However, it is up to the client of the company how they choose to pay, as long as it is paid in full and on time.

If you are thinking of using a debt management company, you should be aware of the following before making your decision:

- Debt management organisations will only be interested in individuals who have some income and can service their debts over time in full-and who own their own home, so that the home can be used as surety against the debts.

- Many debt management organisations will deal only with non-priority debts and leave the individual to deal with priority debts themselves.

- Most debt management companies will charge a fee, typically between £200-250 which leaves less money to pay off the debts. They might also charge a deposit at the outset.

- Most debt management companies also charge a fee to the individual each month, an administration fee. This can be quite high. Remember these companies are in business and you are their product.

- You need to check the contract that you will have with the company and that you can cancel any time if you are not happy. If you can, run any agreement past a Citizens Advice Bureau.

- Debt Management Plans have no legal standing.

Debt management Plans and Credit status

If you are heavily in debt then this is noted on your credit reference file. By entering into a plan with a debt management company, your debts will be cleared based on agreement with creditors. After the agreed payment period is over then your credit status will begin to improve. Negative entries stay on file for six years.

THE PROCESS OF BANKRUPTCY

Chapter 6

The Process of Bankruptcy

Bankruptcy is one way of dealing with debts that you can no longer pay. The bankruptcy proceedings free you from debts which have simply become overwhelming and enable you to make a fresh start, subject to some restrictions outlined later. The process of bankruptcy also makes sure that your assets are shared out fairly between your creditors.

If you have decided that any of the alternatives to bankruptcy outlined in the previous chapters are not for you, and that bankruptcy is your only option, you need to be clear about the process of bankruptcy and what this entails and also the impact that it will have on the next few years following bankruptcy.

Costs of bankruptcy

It is ironic, but it is quite expensive to go bankrupt. In straitened time, this is probably the last thing that an individual needs but there is no escaping the fees. There is, however, the possibility of the courts waiving the fees in certain circumstances, e.g. if you are on income support. It is worth asking the staff at the court whether you are eligible for either waived or reduced fees.

The court fee which has to be sent in with the debtor's petition (see appendix) is currently £150. There is a £360 deposit towards administering your bankruptcy which must be paid in all cases.

In the county court there is the need to swear an affidavit as part of the statement of affairs. This is free if sworn in the county court. However, if your bankruptcy hearing is taking place in the High Court then there is a fee of £7 to swear the affidavit.

If you are married and both you and your spouse are petitioning for bankruptcy, two sets of fees are payable. Fees can be paid by postal order, cash or by building society, bank or solicitor's cheques. Personal cheques are not accepted.

How are you made bankrupt?

A court makes a bankruptcy order only after a bankruptcy petition has been presented. It is usually either presented by yourself (debtors petition-see appendix), or by one or more creditors who are owed at least £750 by you and that amount is unsecured (creditors petition).

In order to petition for your own bankruptcy you need to complete two forms-the petition and the statement of affairs-copies of which can be obtained free of charge from your local county court. They can also be downloaded from the insolvency service website www.insolvency.gov.uk.

The forms, as all county court forms, are numbered, the Petition is form 6.27 of the Insolvency Rules 1986 and the Statement of Affairs is form 6.28. You are required to register to use the Online Form Service. The Insolvency Service Helpline will assist you.

Submitting forms

For online forms, you will be invited to submit them when complete. If an individual changes their mind when the forms are complete then no further action needs to be taken. The forms remain in the system for six months after which they are deleted if no bankruptcy order has been made.

With the actual physical forms you need to take these with you when presenting your petition at court.

Creditor's petition

As stated above, a creditor who is owed over £750 can petition the court for your bankruptcy on the grounds that you cannot afford to pay your debts. The creditor must first serve you with a statutory demand for the money due. If the debt has not been paid or a settlement reached within twenty-one days of the demand then the courts will regard you as being unable to pay your debt and will grant a bankruptcy order.

Where is the bankruptcy order made?

Bankruptcy petitions are usually presented at the High Court in London or at a county court near to where you live, or have traded, within the last six months. A petition can be presented against you even if you are not present in England or Wales at the time. A petition can be brought in circumstances where you are out of the country but have had residential or business connections in England or Wales within the previous three years. Where a government department begins bankruptcy proceedings against you these may begin in the High Court in London or in one of the District registries. However, if you have not lived or traded in London then your case will usually be transferred to the appropriate local county court.

You can get addresses of local county courts from Her Majesty's Court Service Website www.hmcourts-service.gov.uk.

If you are presenting your petition at the county court you will need to take three copies of the completed forms with you on the day of your hearing. If you are dealing with the High Court only one set is needed.

The hearing

On the day of your hearing, the court judge has four different options which he or she may exercise, based on the particular circumstances of your case:

- Stay the proceedings, i.e. delay them if further information is needed before a bankruptcy order can be decided upon.

- Dismiss the petition-this may be because an alternative order such as an administration order will be appropriate.

- Appoint an insolvency practitioner, if it is believed that an IVA is more appropriate.

- Make a bankruptcy order. You will become bankrupt immediately on the making of the order.

The interview may not necessarily be with the judge, it could be with a clerk of the court or the judge may have already decide that a bankruptcy order will be made and the clerk will inform you of this.

After the order has been made you may be shown to an open-plan office where you will be required to speak to the Official Receiver's office, if it is deemed necessary, usually because you have assets that require dealing with immediately. Either a telephone interview will be booked or a time for a face-to-face interview will be booked.

In all other cases the court will inform the Official Receiver that a bankruptcy order has been made. He or she will then act as your trustee in bankruptcy unless the court appoints an insolvency practitioner to act for you.

Assuming that it is the Official receiver who will be acting as your trustee, he or she will be looking after your financial affairs during your bankruptcy and also your financial affairs prior to being made bankrupt. The Official Receiver must also report to the court any matters which indicate that you may have committed criminal offences in connection with your bankruptcy.

A Member of staff from the Official Receiver's Office will contact you within two working days of receiving notice from the court. You may be asked to attend the Official Receiver's office for an interview, normally within ten working days of the order being received. Alternatively, the Official Receiver can suggest a telephone interview, again normally within ten working days of receiving the order. Telephone interviews are normally carried out where you have presented your own petition for bankruptcy, when you have not recently traded, if you have not previously been made bankrupt and where a telephone number for you is available.

Whether you are interviewed personally or by telephone you will receive a letter setting out what is required from you and you may also have to complete a questionnaire.

If a telephone interview has been arranged, the questionnaire will need to be returned by a certain date prior to the interview. If you are being interviewed in person you should take it with you.

You will need to collect together all of your financial records, paperwork generally and any other information that you need for the interview. The following will be needed:

- Financial papers, for example letters, bank statements, bank records, hire purchase agreements, credit card statements and so on.

- The last set of accounts if self-employed.

- You will need to have these available in front of you if you are interviewed by telephone.

- If you are being interviewed in person, you should take the completed questionnaire and the financial records, paperwork and any other information to the interview.

The interview in person

A face-to-face interview will take place in a private room and can last up to 2-3 hours. The questionnaire that you have filled in will be checked and if you have not filled it in you will have to do it then and there. You will then be interviewed by an examiner, a member of staff who is a specialist in insolvency matters, who will go into the details of your assets and debts and the facts and circumstances that led to bankruptcy.

You will be required to hand over all your financial records and papers. They will be examined and recorded then or at a later interview. You should ask any questions about the proceedings or the case when you are at the interview.

Telephone interviews

Telephone interviews are usually much shorter, often lasting little more than half an hour. If you have been offered and have accepted a telephone interview you will be telephoned by the examiner at the agreed time and date. The examiner will start by examining the information in the questionnaire (if you have been asked to complete one) and then will ask you for any necessary additional information about your assets and debts, and the facts and circumstances that led to your bankruptcy. You may be asked to attend another appointment, particularly if:

- The Official Receiver needs more time to complete enquiries into your or your company affairs.

- You cannot, or do not, provide all the financial records requested by the Official receiver.

- They require more details of your assets, debts and financial affairs

- You cannot provide all the information that is needed.

There are certain assets that the Official receiver will let you keep:

- Tools, books, vehicles and other items of equipment which you need to use personally in your employment, business or vocation.
- Clothing, bedding, furniture, household equipment and other basic items that you and your family need in your home.

You will be able to keep these items unless they can be replaced with a suitable cheaper alternative.

The trustee may apply to the court for an order restoring property to him or her if you disposed of it in a way which is unfair to your creditors (for example, if before bankruptcy you had transferred property to a relative for less than its worth). The trustee may claim property which you obtain or which passes to you (for example under a will) while you are bankrupt.

A student loan made before or after the start of a bankruptcy is not regarded as an asset that the trustee may claim, if a balance of the loan is remaining.

If you have made a claim against another person through court proceedings, or you think you may have a claim (a right of action) against another person, the claim may be an asset in the bankruptcy.

After the interview, either in person or by telephone, the Official Receiver will check the information you have given and based on this will issue a report to creditors setting out your assets and debts. This report will usually be issued within eight to twelve weeks of the bankruptcy order being made and the Official Receiver will begin the task of selling any assets that you might have to settle part or all of your outstanding debts. Depending on the type of assets this may take time.

Creditors

After you have been made bankrupt, creditors cannot ask you directly for money. They have to make a claim directly to the trustee. There are some very limited exceptions to this rule:

- Secured creditors, such as creditors who have a mortgage or charge on your home.

- Non-provable debts, such as court fines and other obligations arising under an order made in family proceedings or under a maintenance assessment made under the Child Support Act 1991. Non-provable debts are not included in the bankruptcy proceedings and you are still liable to pay off these debts.

- Benefit overpayments, where the benefit provider can recover any benefit overpayments from further benefits that you receive until you are discharged, when you will be released from these debts.

- Student loans

Payments to creditors

The Official Receiver will tell your creditors that you are bankrupt. He or she may either act as the trustee or may arrange a meeting of creditors for them to choose an insolvency practitioner for them to be trustee. This happens if you appear to have significant assets. You may have to attend the meeting of creditors.

The trustee will tell the creditors how much (if any) money will be shared out in the bankruptcy. Creditors will then have to make their formal claims. The costs of the bankruptcy proceedings are paid first out of any money that is available. Preferential debts are paid first, such as claims by employees (if any) together with interest on all debts. Then the other creditors are paid as far as there are funds available from the sale of your assets. If there is a surplus it will be returned to you. You would then be able to apply to the court for your bankruptcy order to be annulled.

If your trustee makes a payment to your creditors, they may place an advertisement about your bankruptcy in a newspaper asking creditors to submit their claims. Depending on how long it takes your trustee to deal with your assets, this advertisement may appear several years after the bankruptcy order.

If you have provided all the necessary information and dealing with your assets is straightforward you may not hear from the Official Receiver again. If you do not co-operate with the Official receiver's staff, you may have to attend court to be questioned and could even be arrested if you fail to co-operate. You could also have your discharge from bankruptcy proceedings suspended, which would mean that your bankruptcy could last longer than the normal twelve months.

Annulment and the Fast Track Voluntary Arrangement

Annulment of bankruptcy is a procedure whereby a court will cancel the bankruptcy order. An individual can apply to the court for an order of annulment at any time where:

- The bankruptcy order should not have been made, for example because the due process wasn't followed.

- All of your bankruptcy debts and fees and expenses of the bankruptcy have been paid in full or guaranteed to the court.

- You have agreed an IVA with your creditors to repay all or part of your debts.

An annulment means that, legally, a bankruptcy order was never made and you will revert to your status before bankruptcy. However, any disposals of your property by the trustee will be valid and cannot be reversed. Any assets remaining will be returned to you and you will be liable for any debts that have not been paid in the bankruptcy.

Fast Track Voluntary Arrangement

If you have been made bankrupt by one of your creditors but think that you can provide a significantly better return to your creditors than they will receive through your bankruptcy, then by entering into a Fast Track Voluntary Arrangement (FTVA) you can get your bankruptcy annulled.

An FTVA is a binding agreement made between you and your creditors to pay all or part of the money you owe. It can only be entered into after you have been made bankrupt. In order to enter into a FTVA you must secure the co-operation of the Official Receiver, who will act as your nominee. They will help you put together your proposal for your creditors.

For the FTVA to be accepted, 75% of the creditors who vote must agree to the proposal. It is then legally binding, and no creditor can take legal action regarding the debt provided you keep to the agreement. As nominee, the Official Receiver will then supervise the arrangement, making payment to your creditors in accordance with your proposals.

Costs of the FTVA

The fee for acting as nominee is £310. Additionally, for carrying out the ongoing role of supervisor of the FTVA the Official Receiver will charge fifteen per cent of monies from any assets you own or any money collected from you. You will also be required to pay a £10 registration fee for your FTVA to be recorded on the public register of individual voluntary arrangements.

Duration of the FTVA

There is no fixed period for a FTVA. It lasts as long as is agreed and will be outline in the proposal. Once the FTVA has been agreed the Official Receiver will apply to have your bankruptcy annulled, as if it never existed. You will no longer be subject to the restrictions in the bankruptcy order. However, if you fail to comply with the order then the Official Receiver will make you bankrupt again. If the circumstances are beyond your control, such as being made redundant then the Official Receiver will take no action against you. However, your creditors can once again petition for your bankruptcy.

Amending records

Individual Insolvency Register-this will be amended on annulment. It will be your responsibility to have details of your bankruptcy order removed from your credit file. The Official Receiver will also inform anyone who has been informed of the bankruptcy order that the order is now annulled.

Generally...

Your home

If you own your home, whether freehold or leasehold, solely or jointly, mortgaged or other wise, your interest in the home will form part of your estate which will be dealt with by the trustee. The home may have to be sold to go towards paying your debts.

If your spouse and/or children are living with you, it may be possible for the sale of the property to be put off until after the end of the first year of your bankruptcy. This gives time for other housing arrangements to be made. Your husband, wife/partner, relative or friend may be able to buy your interest in your home from the trustee. If the trustee cannot, for the time being, sell your property he or she may obtain a charging order on your interest in it, but only if that interest is worth more than £1,000. If a charging order is obtained, your interest in the property will be returned to you, but the legal charge over your interest will remain. The amount covered by the legal charge will be the total value of your interest in the property and this sum must be paid from your share of the proceeds when you sell the property.

Until your interest in the property is sold, or until the trustee obtains a charging order over it, that interest will continue to belong to the trustee but only for a certain period, usually only 3 years, and will include any increase in its value. The benefit of any increase in value will go to the trustee to pay debts, even if the home is sold some time after you have been discharged from bankruptcy.

Pension rights

A trustee cannot claim a pension as an asset if your bankruptcy petition was presented on or after May 29th 2000, as long as the pension scheme has been approved by HM Revenue and Customs. For petitions presented before May 29th 2000, trustees can claim some kind of pensions. However, given that we are now in 2010, this is not so relevant.

Generally, the trustee will be able to claim any interest that you have in a life insurance policy. The trustee may be entitled to sell or surrender the policy and collect any proceeds on behalf of your creditors. If the life insurance policy is held in joint names, for instance with your husband or wife, that other person is likely to have an interest in the policy and should contact the trustee immediately to discuss how their interest in the policy should be dealt with.

Your life insurance policy

You may want a life insurance policy to be kept going. You should ask the trustee about this. It may be possible for your interest to be transferred for an amount equivalent to the present value of that interest.

If the life insurance policy has been legally charged to any person, for instance an endowment policy used as security for your mortgage, the rights of the secured creditor will not be affected by the making of the bankruptcy order. But any remaining value in the policy may belong to the trustee.

Your wages

Your trustee may apply to court for an Income Payments Order (IPO) which requires you to make contributions towards the bankruptcy debts from your income. The court will not make an IPO if it would leave you without enough income to meet the reasonable needs of you and your family. The IPO can be increased or decreased to reflect any changes in income.

IPO payments continue for a maximum of 3 years from the date of the order and may continue after you have been discharged from bankruptcy. Or you may enter into a written agreement with your trustee, called an Income Payments Agreement (IPA), to pay a certain amount of your income to the trustee for an agreed period, which cannot be longer than 3 years. Each case is assessed individually.

Restrictions on a bankrupt

The following are criminal offences for an un-discharged bankrupt:

- Obtaining credit of £500 or more either alone or jointly with any other person without disclosing your bankruptcy. This is not just borrowed money but any kind of credit whatsoever.

- Carrying on business (directly or indirectly) in a different name from that in which you were made bankrupt, without telling all of those with whom you are doing business the name in which you were made bankrupt.

- Being concerned (directly or indirectly) in promoting, forming or managing a limited company, or acting as a company director, without the court's permission, whether formally appointed as a director or not.

You may not hold certain public offices. You may not hold office as a trustee of a charity or a pension fund. After the bankruptcy order, you may open a new bank account but you should tell them that you are bankrupt. They may impose conditions and limitations. You should ensure that you do not obtain overdraft facilities without informing the bank that you are bankrupt, or write cheques that are likely to be dishonoured.

Ending bankruptcy

If you were made bankrupt on or after April 1st 2004, you will automatically be freed from bankruptcy after a maximum of twelve months. This period may be shorter if the Official receiver concludes his enquiries into your affairs and files a notice in court. You will also become free from bankruptcy immediately if the court cancels the bankruptcy order. This would normally happen when your debts and fees and expenses of the bankruptcy proceedings have been paid in full, or the bankruptcy order should not have been made.

On the other hand, if you have not carried out your duties under the bankruptcy proceedings, the Official Receiver or your trustee may apply to the court for the discharge to be postponed. If the court agrees, your bankruptcy will only end when the suspension has been lifted and the time remaining on your bankruptcy period has run.

Debts

Discharge releases you from most of the debts you owed at the date of the bankruptcy order. Exceptions include debts arising from fraud and any claims which cannot be made in the bankruptcy itself. You will only be released from a liability to pay damages for personal injuries to any person if the court see fit.

When you are discharged you can borrow money and carry on business without these restrictions. You can act as a company director, unless disqualified.

Assets that you obtained or owned before your discharge

When you are discharged there may still be assets that you owned, either when your bankruptcy began, or which you obtained before your discharge, which the trustee has not yet dealt with. Examples of these may be an interest in your home, an assurance policy or an inheritance.

These assets are still controlled by the trustee who can deal with them at any time in the future. This may not be for a number of years after your discharge.

Assets you obtain after your discharge

Usually, you may keep all assets after your discharge.

Bankruptcy restriction orders and undertakings

If, during the enquiries into your affairs, the Official Receiver decides that you have been dishonest either before or during the bankruptcy, or that you are otherwise to blame for your position, they may apply to the court for a Bankruptcy Restrictions Order.

The court may make an order against you for between 2-15 years and this order will mean that you continue to be subject to the restrictions or bankruptcy. You may give a bankruptcy restrictions undertaking which will have the same effect as an order, but will mean that the matter does not go to court.

Debts incurred after you have been made bankrupt

Bankruptcy deals with your debts at the time of the bankruptcy order. After that date you should manage your finances a lot more carefully. New debts can result in a further bankruptcy order or prosecution.

Credit reference agencies

After you have been discharged from bankruptcy, you will want to ensure that you have a clear idea of your credit rating and also that the details that the credit agencies hold on you is correct. The three main consumer credit reference agencies in the UK are Experian, Equifax and Call Credit. They provide lenders with information about potential borrowers which in turn enables the lenders to make their decisions. The agencies hold information about most adults in the UK. However, sometimes this information is out of date, or incorrect in other ways which can adversely affect your credit.

If personal information about you is incorrect or out of date you have the right to change it under the Data Protection Act 1988. You can ask for a copy of your credit report inline or by post from a credit reference agency for £2. You need to provide your name, and any previous name such as maiden name, address and any addresses lived in for the last six years and your date of birth. The credit reference agency must provide you with details within seven working days. The addresses and contact details of each agency are as follows:

Experian 0844 481 8000 www.experian.co.uk

Equifax 0870 010 0583 www.equifax.co.uk

Call Credit 0870 060 1414 www.callcredit.co.uk

Checking the information on your credit file

A bankruptcy will stay on your credit file for six years from the date of your bankruptcy order. You should ensure that the date of your discharge from bankruptcy is correctly shown. If it is not, you should send your certificate of discharge to the agency as proof. Alternatively, a letter of discharge can be obtained from the Official receiver.

Accounts included in your bankruptcy order may show on your credit report as being in default. The date of the default should be no later than the bankruptcy order.

Making a complaint

If the credit reference agency still does not amend the problem after you have contacted them then you can write to the Information Commissioner, who has responsibility for enforcing the Data Protection Act. You should write giving all details of yourself and the problem and they will decide on the action to take. The Information Commissioners Office can be contacted on 0845 630 6060.

Website www.ico.gov.uk

You can, if you so wish use credit repair companies who will, for a fee, undertake checking and rectification of your credit rating.

Conclusion

At the beginning of this book, alternatives to bankruptcy were set out. It was emphasised that these are only any good if you have some sort of income and want a structured approach to managing your debts. For many people this is a suitable alternative to full blown bankruptcy. With the exception of Debt management Plans, the other orders, Debt Relief Orders, Administration Orders and Individual Voluntary Arrangements are formal agreements ratified by the court. These at least keep creditors at bay and help you to clear your debts, or part of your debts, within an agreed timeframe. The Debt Management Plan is rather more informal and carries on until all debts are paid.

Bankruptcy is the final option, where you have no money and need to wipe the slate clean. It is true to say that there is far less of a stigma attached to bankruptcy than there was in the past. Indeed, in the current severe recession for many bankruptcy is the only option, as either business or personal earning dry up.

As bankruptcy lasts for only one year, when the period is over you can pick yourself up and start again. Your credit rating may have been hit but you will be eligible for loans and credit once again. This will be subject to the banks and lenders being satisfied that you can pay off debts in the future.

I hope that this brief book has been of use and good luck in the future. Remember, many famous names have been through the process of bankruptcy and picked themselves up and learnt from experience.

Useful Addresses and Websites

The Bankruptcy Association
Free Post L A 1118
4 Johnson Close
Lancaster
LA1 5BR
Tel: 01539 469474
Email: johnmcqueen@thba.org.uk
www.theba.org.uk

Her Majesty's Court Services (hms)
Lewins Place
Lewins Mead
Bristol
BS1 2NR
Bankruptcy Section
Tel: 0117 910 6726   or 0117 910 6756
Email: enquiries@bristol.countycourt.gsi.gov.uk
www.hmcourt-service.gov.uk

(Bankruptcy Information Centre)
Birkenhead County Bankruptcy Court Information
76 Hamilton Street
Birkenhead
Merseyside
CH41 5EN
Tel: 0151 666 5800
enquiries@birkenhead.countycourt.gsi.gov.uk

Moneymeans
7 Arrowsmith Court

Station Approach
Broadstone
Dorset
BH18 8AX
Tel:08432 899051
www.moneymeans.co.uk

Debt Management, Debt Consolidation, IVA, Bankruptcy, Trust Deeds.
4th Floor The Chancery
58 Spring Gardens
Manchester
M2 1EW1
Freephone: 0800 228 9288
www.chasesaunders.co.uk

Oneadvice
Jadson House
Sibson Road
Sale
M33 7RP
Freephone: 0800 048 1752
www.oneadvice.co.uk

The UK Insolvency Helpline
Consumer and Business Debt Advice Service
Administration Centre
788-790 Finchley Road
London
NW11 7TJ
Tel: 0800 074 6918
www.insolvency.gov.uk

Insolvency Practitioners

Griffin and King
26-28 Goodall Street
Walsall
West Midlands
WS1 1QL
Tel: 01922 722205
www.griffinandking.co.uk
Email: enquiries@griffinandking.co.uk
Their Bournemouth Office
10 Poole Hill
Bournemouth
Dorset
BH2 5PS
Tel: 01202 355348

Their Shewsbury Office
9 Hotspur Street
Shewsbury
SY1 2PZ
Tel: 01743 491239
Email your enquiries to their Licensed Insolvency Practitioners
Tim Corfield at tim@griffinandking.co.uk
Or   Janet Peacock at janet.peacock@griffinandking.co.uk

Insolvency Solicitors and Bankruptcy Lawyers UK Law Firms
Ashford House
Grenadier Road
Exeter
Devon

EX1 3LH
Tel: 0870 7000
www.lawandlegal.co.uk
(This site and address gives you lists of Solicitors and Lawyers)

Ward & Co Insolvency Practitioners
Bank House
7 Shaw Street
Worcester
WR1 3QQ
Tel: 0845 263354
www.companyliquidationworcester.co.uk

The Insolvency Service
The Register of Companies
Companies House
Crown Way
Cardiff
CF4 3UX
Tel: 02920 388588
www.insolvency.gov.uk
Email : sheila.todd@insolvency.gis.gov.uk

Debtsolver
Trafford Plaza
73 Seymour Grove
Manchaster
M16 OLD
Tel: 08000 434 336
Email: info@debtsolver.co.uk
www.debtsolver.co.uk

Citizens Advice Bureau
Helpline 0207 833 2181
www.citizensadvice.org.uk

Community Legal Services
Helpline 0845 345 4345
www.clsdirect.org.uk

Consumer Credit Counselling Service
The CCCS is a registered charity dedicated to providing free, confidential counselling and money management help to families and individuals in financial distress
Helpline 0800 138 1111
www.cccs.co.uk

Consumer Direct
Consumer Direct is the government funded telephone and online service offering information and advice on consumer issues.
Helpline 0845 404 0506
www.consumerdirect.gov.uk

National Debtline
National Debtline provides free confidential and independent advice over the telephone for anyone in financial difficulties.

Helpline 0808 808 4000
www.nationaldebtline.co.uk

Glossary of terms

Administration order-this is an order made in a county court to arrange and administer the payment of debts by an individual.

Annulment-cancellation.

Assets-anything that belongs to a debtor that may be used to pay off debts.

Bankrupt-a person against whom a bankruptcy order has been made by a court.

Bankruptcy-the process of dealing with the estate of a bankrupt

Bankruptcy restriction notice-a notice entered at the Land Registry on any property involved in a bankruptcy.

Bankruptcy order-a court order making an individual bankrupt.

Bankruptcy petition- a request made to the court for a debtor to be made bankrupt.

Bankruptcy restrictions order or undertaking- a procedure whereby the restrictions of bankruptcy continue to apply for between 2-15 years.

Charging order- an order made by the court giving the trustee a legal charge on the bankrupt's property for the amount owed.

Creditor-someone who is owed money by a bankrupt.

Creditor's committee- a committee representing the interests of all creditors in supervising the activities of a trustee in bankruptcy.

Debt Management Plan-an informal arrangement negotiated with creditors by an independent company.

Debt Relief Order-an alternative to bankruptcy for smaller debts.

Debtor-someone who owes money.

Discharge-free from bankruptcy.

Estate-assets or property of the bankrupt which the trustee can use to pay creditors.

Fast Track Voluntary Arrangement-a voluntary agreement with creditors to pay all or part of the money owed, which can only be entered into when bankrupt.

Income payment agreements (IPA) a written agreement where the bankrupt voluntarily agrees to pay the trustee part of his or her income for an agreed period.

Income payments order (IPO)-where the court orders the bankrupt to pay part of their income to the trustee for a period.

Individual Voluntary Arrangement (IVA)-a voluntary arrangement for an individual where a compromise scheme for payment of debts is put to creditors.

Insolvency-being unable to pay debts when they are due.
Insolvency practitioner-an authorised person specialising in insolvency, usually a solicitor or accountant.

Nominee-an insolvency practitioner who carries out the preparatory work for a voluntary arrangement.

Non-provable debt-debt which is not included in the bankruptcy proceedings. An individual remains liable for such debt regardless of his or her bankruptcy.

Official receiver-a civil servant and officer of the court employed by the Insolvency Service, which deals with bankruptcies.

Petition-a formal application made to court by the debtor or creditor.

Preferential creditor-a creditor entitled to receive certain payments in priority to other unsecured creditors.

Public examination-where the Official receiver questions the bankrupt in open court.

Secured creditor-a creditor holding security, such as a mortgage.

Secured creditor-a charge or mortgage over assets taken to secure the payment of a debt. Where the debt is not paid, the lender has the right to sell the charged assets.

Statement of affairs-a document completed by a bankrupt and sworn under oath, stating the assets and giving details of debtors and creditors.

Trustee-either the Official Receiver or an insolvency practitioner who takes control over the assets of a bankrupt.

Unsecured creditor-a creditor who does not hold any security for money owed.

Unsecured debt-a debt owed to an unsecured creditor.

Index

Emerald Publishing
www.emeraldpublishing.co.uk

106 Ladysmith Road
Brighton BN2 4EG

Other titles in the Emerald Series:

Law
Guide to Bankruptcy
Conducting Your Own Court case
Guide to Consumer law
Creating a Will
Guide to Family Law
Guide to Employment Law
Guide to European Union Law
Guide to Health and Safety Law
Guide to Criminal Law
Guide to Landlord and Tenant Law
Guide to the English Legal System
Guide to Housing Law
Guide to Marriage and Divorce
Guide to The Civil Partnerships Act
Guide to The Law of Contract
The Path to Justice
You and Your Legal Rights

Health
Guide to Combating Child Obesity
Asthma Begins at Home

Music
How to Survive and Succeed in the Music Industry

General
A Practical Guide to Obtaining probate
A Practical Guide to Residential Conveyancing
Writing The Perfect CV
Keeping Books and Accounts-A Small Business Guide
Business Start Up-A Guide for New Business
Finding Asperger Syndrome in the Family-A Book of Answers

For details of the above titles published by Emerald go to:

www.emeraldpublishing.co.uk

| Rule 6.41(1) | **Statement of Affairs (Debtor's Petition)** | Form 6.28 |

Rule 6.41(1)   **Statement of Affairs (Debtor's Petition)**   ·Form 6.28

Insolvency Act 1986

NOTE:
These details
will be the same
as those shown at
the top of your
petition
Please complete
this form in black
ink.

In the

In Bankruptcy

No. _____ of 20 _____

Re _____

The 'Guidance Notes' Booklet tells you how to complete this form easily and correctly

Show your current financial position and supply the required information by completing all the pages of this form, which will then be your Statement of Affairs

AFFIDAVIT

When you have completed the rest of this form, this Affidavit must be sworn before a Solicitor or Commissioner for Oaths or an officer of the court duly authorised to administer oaths

I (a) _____

(a) Insert full
name
(b) Insert
occupation
(c) Insert full
address

(b)_____

of (c) _____

_____

_____

Make oath and say that the several pages marked

_____

and contained in the exhibit marked "Z"

are to the best of my knowledge and belief a full, true and complete statement of my affairs at today's date.

Sworn at

Dated this ____ day of _____ 20____ Signature(s) _____

Before me _____

A Solicitor or Commissioner for Oaths or authorised officer

Before swearing the affidavit, the Solicitor or Commissioner is particularly requested to make sure that the full name, address and description of the deponent are stated, and to initial any crossing out or other alterations in the printed form. A deficiency in the affidavit in any of the above respects will mean it will be refused by the court, and will need to be re-sworn.

IN THE   **No**   **of 20**

IN BANKRUPTCY

Re

This is the exhibit marked "Z" referred to in the annexed affidavit of

sworn on the   **day of**   **20**

Before me

Officer appointed to administer oaths

Section 1 :	Personal Details

1.1	Surname	
	Forename(s)	
	Title (Mr, Mrs, Ms etc)	
1.2	Any other names by which you have been known (such as maiden name, alias or nickname).	
1.3	Date of birth	
1.4	Place of birth	
1.5	National insurance number	
1.6	Home address	
1.7	Home telephone number	
1.8	Mobile telephone number	
1.9	On which telephone number can you be contacted during the day?	
1.10	E-mail address	

1.11   Are you (tick all that apply):

Single		Co-habiting		A civil partner	
Married		Separated		A former civil partner	
Divorced		Widowed		A surviving civil partner	

1.12   Are you, or in the last 5 years have you been, involved in proceedings for divorce, separation or the dissolution of a civil partnership?   Yes [ ]   No [ ]

If 'No', please go to question 1.14

If **Yes**, please give details including any
agreed settlement whether formal or
informal, and any gifts or transfers of
property that occurred in those proceedings.

1.13   Name, address and reference of your
       solicitor in the proceedings

1.14   Have you been bankrupt before?

Yes [   ]   No [   ]

If **Yes**, when?

Which court and which Official Receiver's
office dealt with the proceedings?

1.15   Have you previously entered, or have you
       tried to enter, into an Individual Voluntary
       Arrangement (a formal arrangement with
       your creditors, ratified by the Court, to pay
       them in full or part over time)?

Yes [   ]   No [   ]

If **Yes**, give the name and address of the
insolvency practitioner involved and the date
of the arrangement.

1.16   Are you involved in any legal proceedings?   **Yes** ☐   **No** ☐

If **Yes**, please give brief details of the nature of the proceedings, the name and address of any solicitor acting for you, the name of the relevant court and any case or reference number.

1.17   Are you, or in the last five years, have you been a director or involved in the management of a company?   **Yes** ☐   **No** ☐

If '**Yes**', please give details of all the companies in question:

Name of company	If the company is subject to liquidation administration, administrative receivership or other insolvency proceedings, give details of the Official Receiver's office or insolvency practitioner dealing with the company.

Section 2 :	Business Details

Please complete this section if you are or have been self-employed (including a partner in a partnership) at any time in the last two years. If not, go to Section 3.

2.1	What was the name of your business?	
2.2	State the type of business, trade or profession	
2.3	What was the trading address? (this should also be listed in Section 8)	
2.4	Was the business registered for VAT?	Yes ☐ No ☐
	If **Yes**, give the VAT number.	
2.5	If the business was a partnership give the name(s) and address(es) of the partner(s)	
2.6	When did the business start trading?	
2.7	If it has stopped trading, when did it do so?	
2.8	At what address are your books of account and other accounting records kept?	
2.9	If you hold records on a computer, provide details of which records are held, what software is used (including any passwords) and state where the computer is.	
2.10	What is the name and address of your accountant?	
2.11	What is the name and address of your solicitor?	

2.12 Have you employed anybody during the last two
      years?

Yes ☐   No ☐

If **Yes**, do you owe them any money or may any
former employee claim that you owe them any
money, e.g. for wages, holiday pay or redundancy
pay?

Yes ☐   No ☐

⇩

**Details of employees to whom money is
or may be owing should be included in
your list of creditors in Section 4.**

Section 3:   **Assets**

3.1	Details (if none owned write "NONE")	Approximate value £
1. Cash in hand		
2. Cash in bank, building society or similar account		
3. Cash held by anyone for you		
4. Money owed to you		
5. Tools of your trade		
6. Stock in trade		
7. Machinery, plant and equipment		
8. Fixtures and fittings		
9. Freehold land and property		
10. Leasehold land and property		

	Details	Approximate value £
Section 3 cont:	**Assets**	
11. Stocks, shares and investments		
12. Pension policies and other pension entitlements		
13. Endowment and other life policies		
14. Motor vehicles		
15. Farming stock and crops		
16. National Savings and Premium Bonds		
17. Any property or possessions abroad in which you have an interest, including timeshares		
18. Any property or sums due to you under a will or trust		
19. Any other property of any value e.g. paintings, furniture or jewellery		

Section 3 cont:	Assets

3.2 Do you have or have you had any endowment or other life policies? **Yes** ☐ **No** ☐

3.3 If **Yes**, give details, including details of lapsed policies.

Name and address (including postcode) of life assurance company or broker	Policy number	When was it taken out, roughly?	Type of policy	Estimated value of policy £	Name and address (including postcode) of any concern holding security over the policy
			TOTAL	**£**	

3.4 Apart from state benefits, do you have or have you had any personal pension arrangements? **Yes** ☐ **No** ☐

If **Yes**, give details.

Name and address of the pension company	Policy number	Roughly when did you take out the policy? How much have you paid in total?	When are the payments to you due to start?	Amount (if any) being received now, and how often/period £	Value of pension £

3.5 Have you in the last five years given away, transferred or sold for less than its true value any property or possessions you owned? This includes the surrender of life, endowment and pension policies.

Yes ☐   **No** ☐

If **Yes**, please provide the following details.

Description of the asset	When did you give away, transfer or sell the asset?	Name and address of recipient	Estimated market value or true value of the asset	Value at which the asset was given away, transferred or sold

3.6 In the last 2 years have you made any payment to a creditor, other than in the ordinary course of business, with a view to improving the position of that creditor in case you became subject to insolvency/bankruptcy proceedings?

Yes ☐   **No** ☐

If **Yes**, give details.

3.7 Do you own a motor vehicle or have you disposed of any vehicle in the last 12 months? (if you own a motor vehicle, this should also be listed in Q3.1)

Yes ☐   **No** ☐

If **Yes**, please provide the following details:

Make/Model	
Registration number	
Estimated value £	
Finance outstanding £	
Name of finance company	
Reference number of agreement	
Does the vehicle have a valid MOT? If yes, provide expiry date of MOT	
Insurance / Expiry date	
Give your general view on the condition of the vehicle	
Location of vehicle	
Name of any joint owner	

3.8   If you have disposed of any vehicle in the last 12 months, please specify where the vehicle is now.

3.9   Do you have the use of a motor vehicle that you do not own?   Yes ☐   No ☐

If **Yes**, please provide the following details:

Registration number	
Owner	
Estimated value £	

3.10   Has an enforcement officer (previously known as sheriff's officer) / bailiff visited you in the last 6 months?   Yes ☐   No ☐

(An enforcement officer / bailiff is an officer of the court who may attend to remove assets for sale, if, for example, a judgment debt has not been paid)

If **Yes**, please provide the following details:

Name of creditor	Amount of claim £	Date distress levied	Description and estimated value of property seized

Section 4: **List of Secured Creditors**

(e.g. anyone holding a mortgage or charge over property belonging to you)

Name of creditor	Address	Account, reference or agreement number (if known)	Amount owing (A) £	What of yours is claimed and what is its present value? (B) £	Net amount owing (A-B) £
				TOTAL £	

Section 4 cont: **List of Unsecured Creditors**

Name of creditor	Address	Account, reference or agreement number (if known)	Amount owing £	Date incurred	What was the debt for?
			TOTAL £		

Section 4 cont: **List of Unsecured Creditors**

Name of creditor	Address	Account, reference or agreement number (if known)	Amount owing £	Date incurred	What was the debt for?
		TOTAL £			

Section 5 :   Bank Accounts and Credit Cards

Note: Include any current liability also shown in Section 4.

5.1 Do you have any cheque cards, cash dispenser cards,   Yes   No
      credit or charge cards, debit cards, etc?
      ☐   ☐

5.2 If **Yes**, provide details.

Type of card	Card number	Name and address of bank or supplier	Date obtained

                                                               Yes   No
5.3 Are any of the above accounts or cards
      held jointly with anyone else?   ☐   ☐

      If **Yes**, provide details

WARNING:
If you become bankrupt it may be possible for the Official Receiver to ask your bank or building society to release some or all of a credit balance to you if it is required for your domestic living expenses. However you should not access any account without first contacting the Official Receiver. If you become bankrupt, you must not use any credit cards or charge cards and should cut them in half and send them to the Official Receiver.

Note: Include details of accounts with a debit (overdrawn) balance also shown in Section 4.

5.4 Please list any bank, building society or National Savings accounts you hold, or have held in the last two
years, including any joint, business or dormant accounts.

Name and address (including postcodes) of banks etc	Account number	Tick if your regular income is paid into this account	Name of joint account-holder (if applicable)	Balance of account £

Section 6 :	Employment and Present Income

The court can order that you pay part of your earnings or other income to your trustee if your income is more than you need to live on. The order is known as an Income Payments Order and is made under section 310 of the Insolvency Act 1986. Alternatively you can enter into a voluntary arrangement with the Official Receiver or trustee called an Income Payments Agreement under section 310A of the Insolvency Act 1986.

You must answer the following questions about your income and outgoings and you may be asked to provide your wage slips or salary statements and bills such as gas or electricity to support your answers. This will enable a decision to be made as to whether an Income Payments Order or an Income Payments Agreement is appropriate.

The court will not make an Income Payments Order, neither would an Income Payments Agreement be agreed, that would leave you too little income to meet the reasonable domestic needs of you and your family.

If an Income Payments Order or an Income Payments Agreement is made against you, the payments will usually stop after 3 years.

If your income increases while you are bankrupt, you must inform your trustee of the increase within 21 days.

6.1 Are you: employed ☐ self-employed ☐ unemployed ☐

If you are unemployed, when did you last work, what was your last job and who was your last employer?

6.2 If employed, what is your job and who is your employer? What is the address of the personnel department and your pay reference number?
When did you start this job?

If self-employed, give the name and address of the business.

6.3 What is your average monthly take-home pay (include, for example, overtime, commission and bonuses).

£

6.4 How much tax do you usually pay each month?

£

6.5 How much do you pay in National Insurance each month?

£

6.6 Do you receive any other income, including state benefits or tax credits?

Yes ☐   No ☐

If **Yes**, state from what source (for example pension, state benefits, part-time earnings) and how much you receive each month?

£

6.7 How much do other members of your household contribute each month to the household expenses?

£

6.8 Total household income (Q6.3 + 6.6 + 6.7)

£

6.9 Give your current (or last) Income Tax reference number.

Address of tax office (including postcode)

6.10 Do you have any current attachment of earnings orders in force
against you?   **Yes** [ ]   **No** [ ]

If **Yes**, give details

Name of creditor	Date of first payment	Date last payment due	Court	Amount of each payment and whether monthly or weekly £	Total amount paid to date £

Section 7 :	Outgoings

The information in this section may be used to work out how much, if anything, you can afford to pay your creditors each month. It is important that it is accurate and that you include all necessary expenditure.

7.1 How much do you spend each month on the following:-

Mortgage payments or rent on your home

£ _____

Housekeeping (including food and cleaning)

£ _____

Gas, electricity, other heating

£ _____

Water

£ _____

Telephone charges

£ _____

Travelling to and from work and other essential journeys

£ _____

Clothing

£ _____

Maintenance payments and fines

£ _____

Council tax

£ _____

Other essential payments (e.g. life/household insurance, car tax & repairs)

£ _____ → **Provide details of these payments**

Total £ _____

↓

Section 8 :

Current Property
(including properties used for residential and business purposes)

8.1 Give details of any properties you own. (these should also be listed in Q3.1)	Address, type of property (e.g. flat, semi-detached house), number of bedrooms and whether freehold or leasehold	Approximate value of property (A) £	Name and address(es) of any joint owner(s)	Name and address of anyone who holds a charge or mortgage over your property.	Amount owing to each secured creditor (B) £	Net value of the property (A)–(B) £	What insurance is currently in force and what is its expiry date

8.2 Give details of any properties you rent or lease, either alone or jointly.	Address of property	Monthly rent £	Name and address(es) of any joint tenant(s)	Name and address of landlord

You must take or send to the Official Receiver a copy of your lease or rent agreement.
A rent demand or rent book will help if you do not have a copy agreement.

Section 8 cont: **Current Property**

8.3   Apart from properties that you own, rent or lease, are there any other properties in which you may otherwise have an interest?

       Yes ☐   **No** ☐

If **Yes**, give details

Address of property, type of property (e.g. flat, semi-terraced) and number of bedrooms	Who lets you use it?	How much do you pay?	Is there a written agreement?

8.4   Does anyone else have an interest in any of the properties that you own, rent or lease? This interest may be as a sub-tenant, a guarantor of the mortgage, a partner, a joint tenant, joint lessee or otherwise.

       Yes ☐   **No** ☐

If **Yes**, give details

Address of property (including postcode)	Name of person with an interest	Their address, if different from the property (including postcode) and reference	Nature of interest

Section 9 :   Property Disposed of in the last Five Years

	Address of property	Value of property £	When did you sell, transfer or give away the property?	To whom did you sell, transfer or give away the property?	Net sale proceeds (less any charges and legal fees) £	Details of solicitor (name and address) who acted on your behalf in the transaction
9.1 Give details of any properties, owned alone or jointly, that you have sold, given away or transferred in the five years before the presenting of your bankruptcy petition.						

Section 10 :   Members of your Household and Dependents

10.1 Give the names and ages of all
      occupants of your household and
      state which, if any, are dependent
      on you.

10.2 Apart from members of your household,
      is any other person dependent upon you?

Yes   No

If **Yes**, provide details including
their name, address and reason
for dependency

Section 11 :   **Causes of Bankruptcy**

11.1   When did you first have difficulty paying your debts?

11.2   What do you think are the reasons for you not having enough money to pay your debts? You should provide reasons to support your answer. For example, it would not be enough to state "the recession" without explaining its effect on your affairs.

11.3   Have you lost any money through betting or gambling during the last two years?   **Yes**

No

If **Yes**, how much have you lost?

Section 12 :	Declaration

I hereby confirm that my answers to all the above questions (including any extra information on pages following this declaration) are to the best of my knowledge and belief a true and accurate statement of my affairs as at today's date. I understand that I may be committing a criminal offence if I deliberately give false information in relation to my bankruptcy.

Your signature

Name in BLOCK CAPITALS

Date

Section 13 :	Extra Information

Question No.

If there is insufficient space on any page, you should continue your answer to the question on this page. The question number should be given in the left-hand column.

Section 13 cont:	Extra Information

Question
No:

Guidance Notes for Completion of your Statement of Affairs (Debtor's Petition) Form Under Section 272 of the Insolvency Act 1986

IMPORTANT MATTERS TO NOTE

- If you become bankrupt, your bank account may be frozen. If your regular income is paid into any of your bank accounts, you must now make alternative arrangements with your bank and/or Official Receiver for dealing with this income.

- While you remain an undischarged bankrupt, you will not be able to act in the management of a company (unless you apply to the court to do so and are granted permission). If you are a director or otherwise involved in company management, you should take appropriate action to ensure that you are not committing an offence.

- While you are an undischarged bankrupt, it is an offence to obtain credit for more than the statutory amount (currently £500) without first informing the person giving the credit of your bankruptcy.

- While you remain an undischarged bankrupt or are subject to a Bankruptcy Restrictions Order or Undertaking, it is an offence to trade under any name other than the name in which you were made bankrupt without disclosing that name.

- It is essential that you keep all the books and records of account for your business and hand them over to the Official Receiver when requested.

- You must disclose all of your assets. If you fail to do so, you may be committing a criminal offence for which you could be prosecuted.

- The Official Receiver should be kept informed of any change of address if you move before you are discharged from the bankruptcy.

- You are required to inform the Official Receiver if you acquire any property before you are discharged from bankruptcy.

- You are strongly advised to keep a copy of your statement of affairs, including these notes.

- The affidavit can be sworn at the court when you present your petition.

General Points

1. Make sure if you are writing and not typing your answers that you enter all your details in CAPITAL LETTERS (except where your signature is required) and use black ink.
2. You must complete all pages in the Statement of Affairs which apply to you.
3. Where boxes appear which give you a choice of answer, tick those that apply.
4. The information should be accurate at the date of signing and as up to date as possible. If you do not know the precise dates or amounts requested, give approximate dates or amounts and indicate that they are approximate.
5. Give all amounts in the Statement of Affairs to the nearest £. No pence to be shown.
6. Wherever possible, please include postcodes and any reference or agreement numbers.
7. A creditor is somebody you owe money to.
8. A debtor owes you money.
9. Providing FULL details at this stage will assist the Official Receiver and may reduce the need for you to be contacted frequently by the Official Receiver.

Guide to Section 1 - Personal Details

1. Qs. 1.1 – 1.4

   You should provide ALL names by which you have been known and your date and place of birth.

2. Q.1.5

   You will be able to find your National Insurance Number from:

   - your wage slips – these usually have the NI number quoted on them; or
   - your tax returns; or
   - your employer; or
   - your Doctor's Registration Card; or

- your benefit claims/forms.

If you are still unable to find your National Insurance Number you can contact:

The Inland Revenue National Insurance Contributions Office
Benton Park View
Newcastle upon Tyne
NE98 1ZZ

Telephone (0191) 213 5000
Opening Hours: 8.30am to 5.00pm Monday to Thursday, 8.30am to 4.30pm Friday

3.   Qs.1.6 – 1.8

Your current address and contact details must be recorded.

4.   Q.1.9

When entering the daytime contact number please identify whether this is at work, home or another person's telephone number.

5.   Q.1.10

Details of your e-mail address should be provided.

6.   Q.1.11

You should indicate your current status by ticking the appropriate box.

7.   Qs.1.12 – 1.13

You should provide full details of all divorce, separation or dissolution of a civil partnership proceedings you have been involved in the last 5 years including details of any settlements agreed or gifts or transfers made. Details of the solicitor acting for you in these proceedings should be given.

8. Q.1.14

You should provide the full court details of any previous bankruptcies, e.g. Brighton County Court No: 2 of 2002. Where possible you should provide the address of the Official Receiver's office that dealt with any previous bankruptcy order against you but if you do not know the address then just enter the town, e.g. Brighton.

9. Q.1.15

Full details of any Individual Voluntary Arrangement you previously entered should be given including any court details and the name and address of the insolvency practitioner who acted as supervisor of the arrangement.

10. Q.1.16

You should provide details of any legal proceedings that you are involved e.g. divorce proceedings, custody hearings, criminal charges etc.

11. Q.1.17

The Official Receiver will need to establish the details of all companies in which you have been a director. Full details of all the companies you have been involved with, be it as a director or just involved in the management of the company, over the last 5 years need to be provided. If any of the companies you have been involved with are subject to any insolvency proceedings details should be provided including details of the Official Receiver's office or insolvency practitioner's office which dealt with the company.

It is a criminal offence, under Section 11 of the Company Directors Disqualification Act 1986, for a person, who is an undischarged bankrupt, to act as a director (whether formally appointed or not) or be concerned directly or indirectly in promoting, forming or managing a limited company, without the court's permission.

Guide to Section 2 – Business Details

The information in this section is required to build a full history of your self-employment in the last two years.

If you are self-employed, following the making of the bankruptcy order, your business is likely to be closed down and any employees dismissed.

1.   Qs.2.1 – 2.4

The full name of your business should be provided along with the type of business, trade or profession and trading address(es). If your business was VAT registered the VAT number should be recorded.

While you remain an undischarged bankrupt or if you are subject to a Bankruptcy Restriction Order or Undertaking it is a criminal offence for you to carry on business (directly or indirectly) in a different name from that in which you were made bankrupt, without telling all those with whom you do business the name in which you were made bankrupt.

2.   Q.2.5

If your business was a partnership you should state the full name, together with any aliases, and the address(es) of any members of the partnership. The Official Receiver may need to contact any former partner(s) for additional information on matters relating to the partnership business.

3.   Qs.2.6 – 2.7

The period of trading needs to be established. Details of when the business started trading and when it stopped trading need to be provided. If you are unable to provide exact dates then you should provide the month and year.

4.   Qs.2.8 – 2.9

Your accounting records will be required by the Official Receiver and you must ensure that the records are stored safely. Details of their whereabouts should be stated. Additionally if the accounting records are held on computer you should explain exactly what records are held on a computer and give details of the location of the computer. Details of the software used should be provided along with any passwords used.

5.   Qs.2.10 – 2.11

If an accountant or solicitor has acted for you, you should provide their names and addresses and any references used in correspondence. The Official Receiver may need to contact them for additional information.

6.   Q.2.12

If you have employed anybody in the last two years, unless you employed them on a casual basis, you need to tick the appropriate box. If you owe them any money you should also tick the appropriate box and include them in Section 4 as creditors.

Guide to Section 3 – Assets

1.   Q.3.1

All assets you own should be listed, including any business assets e.g. stock in trade. The assets approximate values in £s (not pence) should be recorded in the column on the right hand side. If you do not own a certain asset please write none in the appropriate row.

You will be able to keep the following items unless their individual value is more than the cost of a reasonable replacement:

- tools, books, vehicles and other items of equipment which you need to use personally in your employment, business or vocation;

You must disclose all these items to the Official Receiver who will then decide whether you can keep them.

- clothing, bedding, furniture, household equipment and other basic items that you and your family need in the home.

You do not need to list your clothing or household furniture unless they are of particular value.

The Official Receiver/trustee will take control of all other assets on the making of the bankruptcy order. He or she, or any insolvency practitioner who is appointed as trustee, will dispose of them and use the money to pay the fees, costs and expenses of the bankruptcy and creditors.

2. **Q3.2 – 3.3**

Full details of all endowment policies or life policies held should be recorded here including the policy number, type of policy, approximate value of the the policy and details of any other person who has an interest in the policy e.g. mortgage company, spouse etc.

Generally, your trustee will be able to claim any interest you have in an endowment policy.

3. **Q.3.4**

If you have or have had any personal pension policies full details should be provided.

A trustee cannot usually claim a pension as an asset if your bankruptcy petition was presented on or after 29 May 2000, as long as the Inland Revenue has approved the pension scheme.

If you are receiving a pension or become entitled to do so before you are discharged, the pension is included as income for the purposes of an income payments order or arrangement (see Section 6).

4. **Q.3.5**

If you have sold or given away any of your assets in the last 5 years and received less money than they were worth or no money at all you must provide full details of the transaction.

The trustee may apply to the court for an order restoring property to him or her if you disposed of it in a way which was unfair to the creditors (for example, if before bankruptcy you had transferred property to a relative for less than its worth).

5. **Q.3.6**

If you have made a payment in the last 2 years to any creditor with a view to improve the creditor's position in case you became bankrupt you must provide full details of that payment.

The trustee may apply to the court for an order restoring the position to what it would have been if the payment had not been made.

6.   Qs. 3.7 – 3.8

If you own, or have disposed of any vehicle in the last 12 months, you need to provide full details of the vehicle, its location and an estimate of its value. Details of any outstanding finance should also be provided. If there is any finance outstanding on the vehicle, the Official Receiver will have to contact the finance company to discuss the position.

7.   Q.3.9

If you have use of a motor vehicle that does not belong to you, you must provide details including the owner's name and estimated value.

8.   Q.3.10

Provide details of any visits, within the last 6 months, you have had from the enforcement officer (previously known as sheriff's officer) or bailiff.

If an enforcement officer or bailiff has seized any of your assets you should provide their name and address, details of the creditor they were acting for and what assets were seized. The Official Receiver will contact the enforcement officer or bailiff to obtain the full details of the seizure.

Remember

You must take or send any documents relating to your assets to the Official Receiver. These may include such things as documents of title, share certificates, life assurance documents, endowment policies and pension policies.

Guide to Section 4 – Creditors

The Official Receiver will need to contact all your creditors, as at the date of the bankruptcy order, to tell them you are bankrupt. Full names and postal addresses of everyone to whom you owe money, including any account, agreement or reference number should be given.

1.   Secured creditors are creditors who have a claim over something of yours e.g. mortgage or charge over your home. You need to state the

address of your property in the fifth column in this section. You must also include in the secured creditors list details of any property or goods that are covered by hire purchase agreements.

2. Unsecured creditors are creditors who do not have a claim over something of yours.

3. In the column 'Amount owing' you should provide the best estimate of the amount owed to the creditor.

4. In the column 'Date incurred' you should provide the date of purchase or the date of a loan agreement etc.

5. Examples of debts you might owe include:

Electricity	Gas
Rent	Telephone
Water rates and sewerage charges	Council tax, general rates and community charge
Inland Revenue	Any banks or financial companies
Goods or services you have received	H M Customs and Excise
Guarantees you have given	Department for Work and Pensions
Money owed to employees	Leasing agreements

Customers who have paid money for goods and services that you have not supplied
Creditors claiming their own goods are in your possession

Guide to Section 5 – Bank Accounts and Credit Cards

1. The Official Receiver will need to establish the details of all bank accounts and credit cards held by you either solely or jointly. Full details of all accounts and credit cards held by you either solely or jointly in the last two years should be provided.

2. Any money in your bank accounts at the date of the bankruptcy order will be an asset in the bankruptcy and will be claimed by the Official Receiver. The Official Receiver may release some money to you for necessary domestic expenses. If the account is in joint names, the

Official Receiver will decide how much of the money should be released to the joint account holder.

3. Any money owed to a bank or credit card company is a debt and should be listed in Section 4.

4. All bank accounts are usually 'frozen' by the bank when it becomes aware of a bankruptcy order. You will need to make alternative arrangements for receiving money into your account and paying standing orders, direct debits etc.

5. Q.5.2
    For type of card enter VISA, MasterCard, Switch, Storecard. You must provide the full card number.

    The address of the bank or supplier should be available from your last statement. Where the debt has been purchased or taken over by another firm provide the name of the original supplier, e.g. Barclaycard, but the name and address of the company which has taken over the debt collection.

6. Q.5.4
    You must provide the bank sort code and account number.

Guide to Section 6 – Employment and Present Income

1. Details of your present employment are required to confirm your employment status at the date of the bankruptcy order. Information about Income Payments Orders/Income Payments Agreements are provided in the form. The figures you provide will be used to assess whether an Income Payments Order/ Income Payments Agreement is appropriate. The Official Receiver will not, except in exceptional circumstances, contact your employer.

2. Qs. 6.2 – 6.6
    The details requested about your employer, pay reference number and your average monthly take home pay can be obtained from your wage slips. Ensure you include overtime, commission and bonuses. The amount of tax and National Insurance you usually pay can also be

obtained from your wage slip. Full details of all other income need to be given including all benefits you receive, pension payments etc.

3.   Q.6.7
    Details of amounts that other members of the household contribute each month to the household expenses need to be recorded. If you do not include the contribution of all members of the household you will be unable to claim the full amount of household expenses in the assessment for an income payments order/income payments agreement.

4.   Q.6.8
    To calculate total household income you must add up your monthly income, benefits, pension payments etc and contributions from other members of the household.

5.   Q.6.9
    Your income tax reference number is usually on your wage slip. Your employer will have details of your tax office.

6.   Q.6.10
    Full details of any current attachment of earnings orders in force need to be provided.

Guide to Section 7 – Outgoings

1.   The Official Receiver will need to establish your full financial details. It may be possible that following paying for all your outgoings each month, you will be able to make a contribution to your creditors.

2.   Figures entered should be as close to the actual monthly figure as possible in whole £s (not pence). You may be asked for evidence to support these figures. Make sure you list all your monthly expenditure.

Guide to Section 8 – Current Property

1.   If you own your own home, whether freehold or leasehold, solely or jointly, mortgaged or otherwise, your interest in the home will form part of your bankruptcy estate, which will be dealt with by the Official

Receiver (or an insolvency practitioner appointed in place of the Official Receiver) as trustee of your bankruptcy estate. Your interest in your home may have to be sold to go towards paying your bankruptcy debts. More information on the effect a bankruptcy order will have on your property is available in The Insolvency Service's information leaflet "What will happen to my home?" which is available on the website, www.insolvency.gov.uk.

2.   Q. 8.1
Full details of all properties you own need to be given in the appropriate columns whether you own the property on your own or jointly with another person. The net value of the property is the current approximate value of the property less the amount due to the secured creditor e.g. for the mortgage.

3.   Q.8.2
If you rent your home, the trustee will normally have no interest in the agreement. If you do not comply with the terms of the tenancy agreement, the landlord may take action against you. The Official Receiver may need to tell your landlord that you are bankrupt.

Full details of all properties you rent or lease must be given. The Official Receiver will require a copy of your lease or rental agreement.

4.   Q. 8.3
If you have any interest in or the use of any other property you should provide details of your interest. For example you may have an interest in a property under a will or you may have the use of a property which you pay for but do not have a tenancy agreement for. You do not have to live in a property to have an interest in it, for example you may rent a garage or storage unit.

5.   Q. 8.4
You need to give details of all those persons, not previously mentioned, who have an interest in any of the properties you own, rent or lease. The nature of their interest needs to be recorded.

Guide to Section 9 – Property Disposed of in the last Five Years

1. If you have sold, given away or transferred, in the five years prior to presenting your bankruptcy petition, any properties, owned jointly or solely, you must provide the full details of the transaction.

2. The Official Receiver has a duty to the creditors to report on any and all assets. If you have disposed of any assets (sold, given away, scrapped etc) the Official Receiver needs to establish that this was not done to the disadvantage of the creditors.

Guide to Section 10 – Members of your household and Dependants

1. You may have a relative or friend, who, while living with you or not living with you, is dependent on you for transport, financial assistance etc e.g. elderly/disabled relatives. You should give full details of all those who are dependent on you and provide their address if they do not live with you.

Guide to Section 11 – Causes of Bankruptcy

1. Q. 11.1

    Give the approximate date you first experienced difficulty paying your debts as they became due.

2. Q.11.2

    This is your opportunity to give a short explanation of the circumstances surrounding your current financial position and the reason you are unable to pay your debts.

3. Q.11.3

    The Official Receiver needs to understand the reason for your insolvency. If you have lost money through betting and gambling this may help to explain how you became insolvent. Any losses you have had through gambling, which have contributed to your bankruptcy, should be included here e.g. horse racing, dog racing, casinos.

Guide to Section 12 – Declaration

Your confirmation that all the information you have provided in your Statement of Affairs is true and accurate to the best of your knowledge and belief is required here. You need to sign and print your name and date the declaration.

Guide to Section 13 – Extra Information

Please use these pages to continue your answers where you have had insufficient space to record them in full.

What happens next?

When you have completed the Statement of Affairs, take it to be sworn (or affirmed) before a Solicitor, Commissioner for Oaths or an Officer of the Court.

You will then be able to take your Statement of Affairs together with your petition for bankruptcy to the Court who will set a date for hearing your petition.

Debtor's Bankruptcy Petition
(Title)

(a) Insert full name, address and occupation (if any) of debtor

I

(a)_____

_____

_____

(b) Insert in full any other name(s) by which the debtor is or has been known

also known as

(b)_____

(c) Insert former address or addresses at which the debtor may have incurred debts or liabilities still unpaid or unsatisfied

[lately residing at

(c)_____

_____

(d) Insert trading name (adding "with another or others", if this is so), business address and nature of the business

[and carrying on business as (d) _____

_____

_____]

(e) Insert any former trading names (adding "with another or others", if this is so), business address and nature of the business in respect of which the debtor may have incurred debts or liabilities still unpaid or unsatisfied

[and lately carrying on business as (e) _____

_____

_____

_____

_____

_____]

(f) Delete as applicable

request the court that a bankruptcy order be made against me and say as follows:-

1. (f) [My centre of main interests has been][I have had an establishment] at

_____

OR

I carry on business as an insurance undertaking; a credit institution; ˚ investment undertaking providing services involving the holding of funds or securities for third parties; or a collective investment undertaking as referred to in Article 1.2 of the EC Regulation.

OR

My centre of main interests is not within a Member State

Under the EC Regulation
(i) Centre of main interests should correspond to the place where the debtor conducts the administration of his interests on a regular basis.
(ii) Establishment is defined in the Council Regulation (No 1346/2000) on insolvency proceedings as "any place of operations where the debtor caries out a non-transitory economic activity with human means and goods"

2. I have for the greater part of six months immediately preceding the presentation of this petition (f) [resided at] [carried on business at]_____

_____

(g) Insert name of court within the district of (f) [this court] [(g)   county court]. I am presenting my petition to this court, as it is the nearest full-time county court to (g)
                            county court, for the following reasons:

(h) State reasons (h)

3. I am unable to pay my debts.

4. (f) That within the period of five years ending with the date of this petition:-

(j) Insert date (i) I have not been adjudged bankrupt

(k) Insert name of court **OR**

(l) Insert number of bankruptcy proceedings I was adjudged bankrupt on (j)   in the (k)
Court No. (l)

(ii) I have not (f) [made a composition with my creditors in satisfaction of my debts] or (f) [entered into a scheme of arrangement with creditors] (S16 BA1914)

OR

On (j)   I (f) [made a composition] [entered into a scheme of arrangement] with my creditors.

(iii) I have not entered into a voluntary arrangement

OR

On (j)   I entered into a voluntary arrangement

(iv) I have not been subject to an administration order under Part VI of the County Courts Act 1984

OR

On (j)   an administration order was made against me in the
(l)   county court.

5. A statement of my affairs is filed with this petition.

Date_____

Signature_____

Complete only if petition not heard immediately

Endorsement

This petition having been presented to the court on _____ it is ordered that the petition shall be heard as follows:-

Date _____

Time _____ hours

Place_____

Bankruptcy Order on Debtor's Petition

Rule 6.45

(TITLE)

(a) Insert date

Upon the petition of the above-named debtor, which was presented on (a)

And upon hearing

(b) Delete words in square brackets if no appointment made under section 273(2)

(b) [and upon considering the report of (c)

appointed under section 273(2) of the Insolvency Act 1986]

(c) Insert name of insolvency practitioner appointed under section 273(2)

And upon the petition and statement of affairs

It is ordered that (d)_____

(d) Insert full description of debtor as set out in the petition

be adjudged bankrupt.

[And it is ordered that (e) _____
be appointed trustee of the bankrupt's estate]

(e) Only to be completed where a trustee is appointed on the making of the bankruptcy order under section 297(4) or (5) of the Insolvency Act 1986

[And it is also ordered that _____]

(f) And the court being satisfied that the EC Regulation does apply declares that these proceedings are (g)_____ proceedings as defined in Article 3 of the EC Regulation

(f) Delete as appropriate
(g) Insert whether main, secondary or territorial proceedings

OR

(f) And the court is satisfied that the EC Regulation does not apply in relation to these proceedings.

Dated _____

Time _____ hours

Important Notice to Bankrupt

(h) Insert address of Official Receiver's office

(f)[The] [One of the] official receiver(s) attached to the court is by virtue of this order receiver and manager of the bankrupt's estate. You are required to attend upon the Official Receiver of the court at (h)

_____

immediately after you have received this order.

The Official Receiver's offices are open Monday to Friday (except on Holidays) from 09.00 to 17.00 hours

Endorsement on Order (j)

(j) Order to be endorsed where debtor is represented by a solicitor

The solicitor to the petitioning debtor is:—

Name _____

Address _____

Telephone No. _____

Reference

Proof of Debt – General Form

(TITLE)	
Date of Bankruptcy Order	No.

1	Name of creditor (If a company please also give company registration number).	
2	Address of creditor for correspondence.	
3	Total amount of claim, including any Value Added Tax and outstanding uncapitalised interest as at the date of the bankruptcy order.	
4	Details of any documents by reference to which the debt can be substantiated. (Note: There is no need to attach them now but the trustee may call for any document or evidence to substantiate the claim at his discretion as may the official receiver whilst acting as receiver and manager, or the chairman or convenor of any meeting).	
5	If amount in 3 above includes outstanding uncapitalised interest please state amount.	£
6	Particulars of how and when debt incurred (If you need more space append a continuation sheet to this form).	
7	Particulars of any security held, the value of the security, and the date it was given.	
8	Particulars of any reservation of title claimed, in respect of goods supplied to which the claim relates.	
9	Signature of creditor or person authorised to act on his behalf	

Name in BLOCK LETTERS

Position with or in relation to creditor

Address of person signing (if different from 2 above)

Admitted to vote for	Admitted for dividend for
£	£

Date	Date
Official Receiver/Trustee	Trustee